HOW TO SAVE
the World

POETRY ANTHOLOGY
TO FIGHT HUNGER

**ALL PROCEEDS
DONATED TO FIGHT
WORLD HUNGER!**

HOW TO SAVE
the World

- POETRY ANTHOLOGY TO FIGHT HUNGER -

5310
PUBLISHING

Published by
5310 Publishing Company
Go to 5310publishing.com for more great books.

Our books may be purchased in bulk for promotional, educational, or business use. Please contact your local bookseller or 5310 Publishing at sales@5310publishing.com.

How to Save The World - Poetry Anthology to Fight Hunger
ISBN 9781990158018 (ebook)
ISBN 9781990158001 (paperback)

Modern and contemporary poetry
POETRY / Anthologies (multiple authors)
POETRY / Subjects & Themes / Inspirational
POETRY / Subjects & Themes / General

Prepared for Publication by 5310 Publishing
Cover design by Eric Williams

Plant illustrations from vecteezy.com
Flower elements from freepik.com

SCAN ME

About 5310 Publishing

We are changing the world!

What once started as a dream soon became a reality — we are proud to give a chance to all writers and storytellers to tell their story, share their cultures, and bring their imagination to life.

5310 Publishing is home to original and skilled authors who want to cause a positive impact.

We publish stories that readers can relate to. We help writers who want to help, encourage, and heal others. Always looking for people who want to transform society and their community, 5310 Publishing believes that innovation starts with us, and only we have the capability to build a better future.

We are a family-owned business dedicated and committed to helping our authors get their books published and to discover new and original ways of promoting their stories and views in front of an audience.

By staying ahead of the competition, embracing new technologies, and collaborating with authors at almost every stage of the publishing process, we do our best to promote and sell our books around the globe.

We are committed to helping the world as well as local communities. We want to develop a more welcoming, diverse, and tolerant world by bringing original and impactful stories to audiences worldwide.

About This Project

How to Save the World: Poems to Fight Hunger

There are more than 820 million people in the world that have insufficient food and other substances for good health and condition. Undernourished kids, hunger and malnutrition are the number one risk to health -- greater than AIDS, malaria, and tuberculosis combined.*

*Data from the United Nations

We have a commitment to help those in need.
We are all human.

As a result, besides publishing impactful and inspirational stories, 5310 Publishing also took part in different projects to help better life on Earth.

As of 2021, 5310 Publishing has donated more than a thousand meals to families in need around the world.
A thousand meals is not enough to help millions of people, but it is a start!

In 2018 we had a dream: to end hunger.
That dream hasn't changed.

With this book, we want to end hunger with poems! "How to Save the World" includes poems about what we want the world to be, how it can be a better place, things we can do improve, how things have been bad but are getting better, and much more!

Worsening economies, climate emergencies, and COVID, are pushing more and more people into starvation.

All proceeds from this anthology will be donated to various food programs to fight hunger!

We will pick a different charity, food program, nonprofit, and/or food bank to donate from time to time, please refer to our website for the most up-to-date information about our efforts.

531OPUBLISHING.COM/HOWTOSAVETHEWORLD

About The Authors
and their social media handles

The authors who contributed to this anthology are donating all of their royalties to the fight hunger as part of our mission! All authors contributed with original poems. Please follow the authors on social media if you want to support them and learn more about what they do. Thank you.

@5310publishing	-	**5310 Publishing**
@eric5310pub	-	**Eric Williams**
@baileygeepoetry	-	**Bailey Gee**
@CatWebling	-	**Cat Webling**
@coriwrote	-	**Cori Nevruz**
@ShatzDaniel	-	**Daniel Shatz**
@WriterRavenclaw	-	**Diana Coombes**
@laliaristo	-	**Lali A. Love**
@iammalicool	-	**Malcolm Whitby**
@MQuigley1963	-	**M.A. Quigley** (Melisa Quigley)
@LashariNeelam	-	**Neelam Lashari**
@AikinNorb	-	**Norb Aikin**
@PoeticallySp45	-	**Rachael DK**
@RS_Rutherford	-	**R.S. Rutherford**
@TheGiftOfLife19	-	**Sean Stevens**
@skyboivin2	-	**Sky Boivin**

Eric Williams is the owner of 5310 Publishing. 5310 Publishing publishes, services, and distributes books and ebooks worldwide. 5310 Publishing is a family-owned business dedicated and committed to helping our authors get their books published and to discover new and original ways of promoting their stories and views in front of an audience. Follow @eric5310pub on Twitter and @ericbookpublisher on Instagram. Follow us @5310publishing on Twitter and Instagram.

Bailey Gee has been writing since she was a small child, as she was in hospital for surgeries and procedures. Writing was always an escape for her. She began writing short stories, and didn't fall in love with poetry until much later in her high school years. It was a teacher who told her "poetry doesn't have to rhyme". From that moment on, Bailey was hooked on poetry. She graduated from George Brown college with a certificate in creative writing. Bailey has entered and won several poetry contests. Her proudest accomplishment to date, is being the author of two books. Bailey has taken her experiences living with mental health issues and physical disability, and has turned them into beautiful books of poetry. She receives praise from all over, Telling her how her books have helped people. Bailey is currently working on her third book and is ready to take the world by storm. @baileygeepoetry

Cat Webling is an author and actress based in Kansas, having recently moved from Georgia. She's been telling stories since she was a little girl, to anyone who would listen. Now those stories just happen to be a bit bigger. She's a lover of all things magic and macabre, strange and surreal, and of course, anything to do with space. Sci-fi and fantasy are my jam, as are video games and TTRPGs! Beyond writing, Cat loves to read, act, cook, play video games, and cuddle with her one-eyed wonder cat or her son, not necessarily in that order. @CatWebling

Cori Nevruz is the author of the thrillers "Left Without Answers" and "Dirty Laundry." Cori likes to write emotionally invested suspense that readers can connect with. "Dirty Laundry" tells the story of Samantha, a suburban housewife who goes into extremes to keep her secrets private. Samantha goes into extremes to keep the life that she's always dreamed of. Will sharing secrets with this newfound friend put them both in danger from Samantha's very private and controlling husband? "Left Without Answers" is an intriguing suspense about Alice as she goes on a desperate search for answers regarding her son's death. When Alice starts finding sticky notes that could only be from her dead son, her desire for revenge intensifies along with her desperate search for the truth. Can Hank's notes provide the answers Alice is seeking before she completely unravels? As Alice searches for answers and closure, the more she learns about Hank's secret life, the more she feels Left Without Answers. Originally from Raleigh, North Carolina, Cori Nevruz now resides in Wilmington with her husband and three sons. She has also previously published the thriller "Making a Killing" and eleven children's books that feature student illustration, giving over 100 children published illustrator credit. She is an active volunteer at her boy's schools, is an avid reader, potty humour enthusiast, and strong believer in the power of kindness. @coriwrote and @coriwroteabook

About **Daniel Shatz**: "I can't remember a time in my life when I wasn't reading or writing. Whether it was screenplays, poems, music, or a fantasy series… A few years back, I had a dream that haunted me. It was a long story of two friends, one of whom saved the other from evil. That dream has now evolved into "The Eighth Renewal" series. It's been a long and fun journey. I live in and love New York State. When I am not writing, usually I am harassing my wife and my son to the point of insanity. I am an avid poker player, music lover, hiker and video game player." @ShatzDaniel

Diana Coombes has always loved writing, from poems, short stories, and fictional novels. Her latest book, *It Won't Happen Again,* was published on April 12th 2021. Her novel is about a woman, who is a victim of a controlling husband. To her neighbours her world is perfect. They think he is a generous man, but to Martha he is only generous with his negativity. Can she turn from a victim and rise from the ashes? @WriterRavenclaw

Lali A. Love is an award-winning author and Amazon bestseller of dark fantasy, science fiction, paranormal thriller, and metaphysical poetry. She has received the NYC Big Book Gold Award for Poetry Anthology, a Global e-Book Gold Award, the Elite Choice Gold Award, the Book of Excellence Award, the Queer Indie Lit Youth Gold Award, and the International Reader's Favorite Bronze Award for quality and powerful storytelling. Her mission is to empower, enlighten, and entertain her readers by bridging the concepts of spirituality with gripping visionary fiction. Lali aspires to write stimulating, inclusive, thought-provoking, and relevant character-based novels that relate to modern-day issues and invoke an emotional response in her readers. She has studied epistemology and metaphysics to further her understanding of the Universal Laws of Energy. As an intuitive, alchemist, and energy healer, Lali intends to help elevate levels of consciousness by shining the light on sensitive subject matter to assist individuals in their healing journeys. She is an advocate for self-love, self-actualization, voicing authentic truths, equality, diversity, unity, women, and children. @laliaristo

Malcolm Whitby is a content creator, artist, author, gamer, and poet. @iammalicool

M.A. Quigley (Melisa Quigley) is an award-winning author of *the Complexities of Love*, dubbed by Lambda Literary "The Most Widely Anticipated Young Adult LGBTQ+ Literary Fiction" and Kirkus Reviews as "Intriguing and Messily Realistic." Melisa was born and raised in Victoria, Australia. She has an Associate Degree in Professional Writing and Editing from RMIT University in Melbourne, Australia. Her work has been published in anthologies in America, Australia, India, and the Philippines. The Complexities of Love, a young adult coming-of-age romance, is her debut novel, and is available worldwide. Follow @MQuigley1963 on social!

Neelam Lashari is an Internationally Published Writer and a Bilingual Poet. She is a co-author of many international anthologies. She had an experience of writing in many magazines and on digital platforms. She likes to play with words that can portray a common man and their issues. @AikinNorb

Norb Aikin is an award-winning poet. @AikinNorb

Rachael DK was born and raised in the United States on the East Coast. She comes from a large and loving family. When she wasn't busy with family time, she spent her days writing poetry, reading her favorite books, and playing board games. Out of necessity, she started educating herself about Mental Health in her late teens and has advocated for herself ever since. Years later she worked in the public libraries where her love of books and people could truly flourish. There is where she met her future spouse—a fellow booklover. Together for almost two decades, they raise their children with the same love of learning and imagination. Rachael is a poet, a bookworm, a wife, a mother of two, a mental health advocate, a breast cancer survivor, autoimmune disease thriver and much more! @PoeticallySp45

R.S. Rutherford is a writer. @RS_Rutherford

Sean Stevens is a father of four and avid writer. While his main genre is poetry he enjoys writing short stories as well. Sean was raised in the inner city right outside of Boston. He enjoys traveling and using his words to help people heal. @TheGiftOfLife19

Ski Boivin was born in Worcester, Mass. She is a poet of multiple anthologies and a mom of two great and imaginative kids. Her oldest is in college and her youngest still keeps her on her toes. @skyboivin2

Acknowledgements

by Eric Williams, owner of 5310 Publishing

Thank you to all the authors who donated their poems to be part of this project. People rarely think of others in need, but you guys thought about all the families around the world who need our help and took the time to write something special just for them.

We can't thank you authors enough for helping us put this together, I am very grateful and I know that the families receiving the donations will also be grateful.

Special thanks to Sky Boivin, who contacted me multiple times at different occasions to submit different poems and also invited some of her friends to participate. May you continue to be this special person, always thinking of others even though you and your family have your own struggles... I know that your writing will keep inspiring others for years to come. You will get far! So, thank you!

Lastly, thank you to you, dear reader, for supporting our project. We have big dreams, and they are only possible because of you. You're awesome-sauce.

Thank you,

Eric Williams, publisher

Save The Nest

by Eric Williams

In this book of rhymes
We're saving lives
We're doing our best
To be the best
To save the nest
So we won't need a next

Because we're here now
Let's all make a vow
To write a word
To change the world

Who's the next that will
Be paying the bill?
We all have free will
So let's not kill

Asking for nothing in return,
Watching all this wood burn
We're always doing the wrong thing
Never cared for your next of kin

But we're here now.
The time is now.
Let's do it.
Let's get loud.

I'm writing this poem
To save a life
To plant a tree
And to feed a kid

The future starts with us now
We're here, let's make a vow
We'll do out best to be the best
Let's do our best to better the nest

This is not a test,
This is reality
Let's start it now
You already know how.

Let's all make a vow
To write a word
To change the world

Be the best.
Save the nest.
So we won't need a next.

by M.A. Quigley

Roaming the streets
No home
No food
Nowhere to go
Sleeping on a park bench
Being told by a policeman
You'll have to move
Begging for money
To buy something to eat
And drink
People walk past
I can hear their comments
They're not very nice
Feeling vulnerable
Wanting support
No self-esteem
I was once an office worker
Just like them
They don't know my story
I don't know theirs
If only they'd open
Their hearts, minds and ears
It would bring comfort
Instead of fear

Stand and Celebrate
by Cat Webling

We stand in the fading light
Of evening as another day closes
I smell the sweet summer perfumes
Of sea salt air and roses

For today we celebrate
We feast and laugh and dance
We take the time this bright evening
While we still have the chance

We know that on the horizon
Another storm approaches
And with it comes the feeling that
The longest night encroaches

And knowing now that in the dawn
We will start the descent into
The cold and dark of coming winter
Still, this much is true

Times will come that shake us
And hurt us to our very soul
The years will pass, taking with them
Their vast, inevitable toll

We'll know that though it's hard
To guess, this much is known
We will face trials and tribulations
But we will not stand alone.

After The Storm

by Cori Nevruz

There are storms in life that leave
your world turned upside down.
Whether literal or figurative,
it will leave you with a frown.

But look out for the light that follows
storms closely behind,
the neighbours, friends and family
chipping in and being kind.

They'll offer thoughts and prayers
and even sometimes a meal or two.
They clean up and rebuild
and give a boost to push you through.

If you need a happy thought
to help you sleep and to feel warm,
rather than look for the damage,
see the light after the storm.

Come Home To Me

by Lali A. Love

Imagine a place
of warmth and tranquility.
A field of eclectic realms,
holding each other's hand with agility.

Dancing together
in joyful bliss,
Our hearts embrace
with Divine's blessed kiss.

Hear the harmonious
sound waves of humanity,
Humming at the vibration
of connected community.

Enveloped by elation and the pureness
of childish giggles,
Our compassion and kindness
are celebrated with wiggles.

We become one, unified in wholeness
with the Source above,
Flowing back home to the rapture
of our heart-centered love.

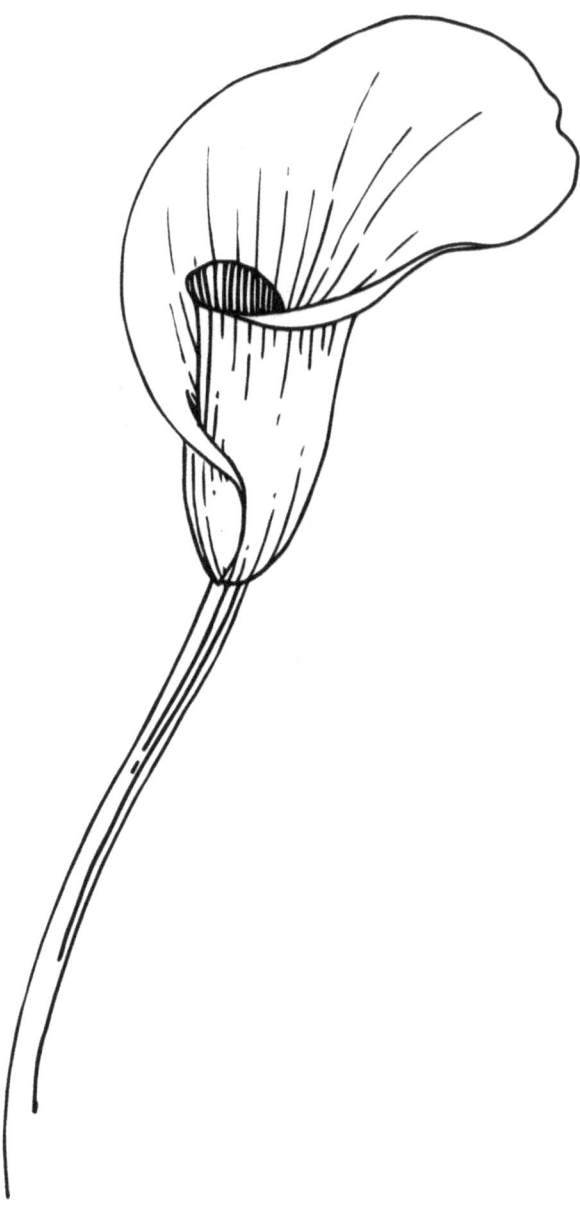

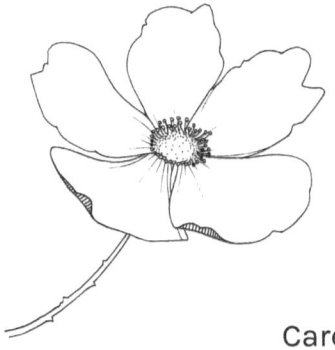

Climate Control
by Diana Coombes

Care of the earth.

Let us do more.

Inspiration to others.

Mother planet to the fore.

All of us together.

Then we can change forever.

Earth can stand no more!

Creation so clever.

Our precious home will heal.

Nothing should stop us.

Trying to keep it real.

Recycle paper and plastic.

Our options fantastic.

Love will seal the deal!

Food for All

by Sean Stevens

Pray for the hungry
How could this be?
A world full of riches
Yet some without wheat

Stomachs are empty
Hearts are now cold
Accepting of all
Walking by slow

Assume someone else
Will take upon ways
Carry this challenge
Whilst you walk away

We all share this journey
Together we form
United as one
To shelter the storm

Please share upon hands
Guide toward light
Help fight this hunger
Children we right

For none should feel hopeless
Together we breathe
Human in nature
Comfort believe

I now share a message
This story is told
The hearts of us all
Will fill the new role

Reach with your soul
Help those who in need
Bring justice to hunger
For hope we are free

Psalms 23

by the Book of Psalms

The Lord is my shepherd; I lack nothing.

He makes me lie down in green pastures.
He leads me beside still waters.

He restores my soul. He guides me in the paths of
righteousness for his name's sake.

Even though I walk through the valley of the shadow of
death, I will fear no evil, for you are with me.

Your rod and your staff, they comfort me.

You prepare a table before me in the presence of my
enemies. You anoint my head with oil. My cup overflows.

Surely goodness and loving kindness
shall follow me all the days of my life,
and I will dwell in the Lord's house forever.

The Broken Compass
by Sky Boivin

Give us your tired
Your huddled masses
Your poor
Those who you do not adore
Give us them all
Send them along their way
We welcome them
With opened arms
Wide and inviting
Like a family member
Long lost gone
And now returned home again
At least that is how
we used to be
Once upon and Long ago
Narcissism has now overrun
Taken ahold
Greed and vengeance
Ridicule as well
How long?
How long,
Until we return to once before?
Such a great country
Stood strong once before

Togetherness
Arm in arm
Brother to brother
Sister to sister
We stood tall as one
But divided a country
We have grown to be
Weak in the eyes of the world
Sorrow and pity
Is looked upon us now.
A new found hope
Shines bright in the horizon
A new era
A new time
The world rejoices
alongside us now
Now is a new beginning
A time to rebuild
A once great country
Back to our roots
Back to family bonds held strong
Morals to be found
Once again
Let us right
The broken compass
That we have become

Divided

by M.A. Quigley

Paths cross

And intertwine

Misunderstandings happen

About hatred, terror,

Religion, race and colour

Morning, noon and night

Don't speak of love

Speak of understanding

And reconciliation

Because all lives matter

Embrace
by Lali A. Love

Sacred Goddess, how you inspire with your connectivity
Birthing and cultivating your soulful creativity.

Nourishing me with your tender embrace
Loving me endlessly without disgrace.

Teaching me patience and vulnerability
Honor, humility, and heartful sincerity.

Ready to receive revitalization and infinity
Balancing your celestial counterpart with Divinity.

A melody sung since the beginning of time
Intertwined as a twin flame dance in an endless rhyme.

Embracing your inner warrior that you forgave
With both spirits strong, devoted, and brave.

Interconnected in the Cosmos with profound unity
Worthy to be cherished and supported as a loving
community.

Before The World Changed

by Cori Nevruz

before the world changed,
there were fires in the streets,
hate speech in the tweets,
and people wore sheets

before the world changed,
women sought fair treatment,
still physically different,
but earn cent for cent

before the world changed,
you loved who they said
two women couldn't wed
or two men love instead

before the world changed,
you were judged by your skin,
tone races stayed with their own,
and hatred was well known

before the world changed,
your religion could cause hate,

your cross carried weight,
your hijab sealed your fate

but, then the world changed.
we were no longer daunted.
we loved who we wanted,
uniqueness we flaunted.

and with the world changing
we helped one another
every man was our brother
we worked with each other

and now the world's new,
we don't always agree.
you're you, and I'm me
yet, we still live in peace.

At The Root of Hope

R.S. Rutherford

Dark

Buried deep

Down in the dirt

Deeper than the dead sleep

Where light does not touch or dare dream to reach

A claustrophobic shell

A wall of self-preservation

Squeezed tight like fists of coal praying for palms of
diamonds

Tears shed down like cascades of wilted petals

Nourishing a dull ache that looms and lingers in the
chest

Struggling in a self-made prison of lonely isolation,
begging for the Sun

Writing letters never sent, to a you that exists no more,
as you wait for anything to save you from this waking
nightmare

Dreams cannot break you free, there is no escape from
the confines placed upon you, sheltering you in place

Stretch

Release

It's not much, but it brings a relief you never knew you
couldn't live without
The walls crack and split and though darkness remains
you can breathe a little now
That loneliness at home in your chest takes flight with
every stretch, with every crack breathing in air
Pushing through the darkness and dirt, swimming in an
ocean of earth as you set your sights on the surface
Though you wish for it to burst forth all at once, it does
not, time takes its toll from you as you wait, and wait,
and wait
Stretching ever more closer, reaching out with hands
ready to accept the dawn
You're cracked and broken and falling to pieces, but from
that loss springs life as you push through the surface,
through the darkness that was your life, through the pain
you never believed you could endure
Out into the Sun, washed in light and renewed, welcomed
by the sweet scent of freedom
A brightness once lost now returned as you grow, aimed
towards the sky as you climb higher
Screaming through all you've left behind, the shackles
you've worn released, rusting away the higher you ascend
Closer to being you again, but not you, a stronger you, a
you that now knows they can face the worst life has to
throw at them and survive

Your limbs take shape, grasping opportunity in every direction, greeting the possibilities of tomorrow
The waters may fall upon you, but now you may embrace them for they are not carried on darkness, let them cleanse you of all that has come before you, ingrain the memory on your skin as a reminder, that's where you've been and where you're going is endless
The clouds make way as you climb, rising higher, towering over the land, gazing down at what seemed like the end, little did you know it was only the beginning
The Sun is shining, the skies are clear, and the future is bright, and it came from within, at the heart of you, when your lowest felt like it would never end, when tomorrow meant nothing, you pushed on and broke free, from a tiny seed came a mighty oak, and at its core is the root of hope.

Stand Together

by Neelam Lashari

The world
It's not just
A word

it's not just
A combination
Of few alphabets

The world is a
Beautiful place

Let's make it better
The best place to live in

Let's join hands
To live together

Let's help
Each other
To live equally

Let's stand together
In every situation
For our children

Let's help everyone
Let's help the poor
Let's help the needy

Let's make the world
A better place to live in

Protesting
by Rachael DK

We have a choice
to silently watch others' fears.
Some may cry, some may shout.

Others pretend all civil rights
will just work itself out.

Or they go on with their activity
not giving it the time of day.

Kneeling for prayers behind
their closed doors at home,
but to friends have nothing to say.

Quiet and unbothered by
bigotry shown to men and women.
Then seeing more murders
provoked by racism towards some citizens...

I may leave this place of
my own volition,
if these fair-weather friends

all decide to stay.

I'll keep helping my own communities

and keep on writing what I need to say.

We can never give up,

stay down, or step aside.

Because we care for all humanity,

while loving who we are on the inside.

Cage

by R.S. Rutherford

A cage did once surround my being

Devouring

De-powering

Swallowing

Hollowing

Till all it left behind was…me

But not me

Me without me

Me inside me

Me beside me

Me twisted, broken, shattered, pummeled,

face down and disgraced

A mirror that cracks is still you reflected back

Beyond the coldness of these bars I saw a sight so

brazen and bold

A vision I felt unfit to behold

A bird

A bird beyond this cage

A bird flying high

A bird without a care

A bird not knowing it should not fly

Those clouds were not made for you to climb so far out of

reach of the filth-ridden hands glaring up from below

Envious

Traitorous

Disgusted by the flaunting of such freedom

My hands wrap around these rusted bars

My nails scrape against their decaying form

My blood boils over and paints me red

Anger is my only friend

And it is visited by jealousy, pity, and despair often

If only I could stretch out and grasp that freedom

If only I could take flight

If only I....

Wait...

Everything feels so far away

The wind carries me higher

I steady my vision and gaze with eyes open wide

Bewildered by my empty cage below

Was it ever really mine?

Was I ever really there?

Or was it all inside of me...

For I am the bird

I am free

I am miles from that cage

And with these wings outstretched, aiming for the sun, I

fly with hope towards endless possibilities

Craving the Light
by Malcom Whitby

Engulfed in hate, the world sinks into darkness
Blanket by death and sorrow, the world hungers
Craving for the light, will you
sweep away our unkindness?

In life we plea to the leaders to exercise awareness
To see the people through the eyes
of empathy not just the numbers
Engulfed in hate, the world sinks into darkness

Controlled by the system the media leave us brainless
Ignoring the truth, hidden among the system blunder
Craving for the light, will you
sweep away our unkindness?

Looking to heaven for freedom
but tuck in earth in blindness
Searching for a way out
following the map to eternal slumber
Engulfed in hate, the world sinks into darkness

Blanket in the depth of despair
questioning their 'gods', whom are nameless
How can we save our planet
while savaging for earthly plunders?
Craving for the light will you
sweep away our unkindness?

History states the world will get
its routine cleaning process
To wash away the muck of the earth,
how can we dampen our hunger?

Craving for the light will you
sweep away our unkindness?
Engulfed in hate,
the world sinks into darkness.

We Are Hope
by R.S. Rutherford

Gaps between a breach of nothingness
Endless in a greying void of nowhere
What finds its way within may nevermore escape
The light, though warm, cannot reach this place

It's cold here
Damp, desolate,
devoid of the brightness of color,
the fullness of life

An angry apathy resides where it is not wanted
The sounds of living disturb
the cornered shadows taking roost

I wake to sleep, and sleep to never wake
Is this my grand defeat?
Perhaps...
But...
No...
Wait...
A crack?
A sliver?
A break?
Hope.

Through these clouded walls
of uncertainty and doubt,
through darkness
so thick it blinds the night

We find hope
Chipping away at the fragile frame
of this silent scream encapsulating
Piece by piece by piece by piece by piece
Defiant in its unrest
Persistent in its desire for change
Hear me now, oh great hopeful wish,
deliver us from the depths of ourselves
and raise us up to heights once known
Push us beyond beyond
Move us to our very core
Bring us to our knees
only to pull us up again
We are not waiting for salvation,
for it is here, it is us
Release us from this chain of limitations and stand back
as we exceed your expectations

We are the now.
We are tomorrow.
We are hope.

Everyday Kindness

(from the book *Everyday Kindness*, *1st Ed.*, *by Cori Nevruz*)

It is a better feeling to give than to receive you'll find.
And every day is a fresh chance to show you can be kind.

Bake a special treat for someone in your neighbourhood.
Treating someone kindly will make you both feel good.

Write a nice note on the sidewalk for all who pass your way.
You'll bring a smile to their faces
and maybe even make their day.

A new outfit or toy for a child that is in need.
Donate to a school a book that you no longer read.

Do a chore for mom and dad before they even ask.
You'll feel all warm and fuzzy
when you're finished with your task.

Volunteer with your family at a local food bank.
Help your brother or your sister
clean the family fish tank.

Compliment a friend or even someone you don't know.

Spend time with a grandparent,
let them teach you how to sew.

Say thank you to a teacher who does so much for you.
You can even write a note and draw a picture, too.

Make a gift for someone that you create special by hand.
Treat your neighbours to a free warm up
at your hot chocolate stand.

Kindness is contagious,
so pass it on today.
Your kind words and actions
will soon come back your way.

Dear Disabled girl

by Bailey Gee

Dear disabled girl,
You are beautiful,
Every part of you.
Every disabled, beautiful part of you.

That wheelchair,
That walker,
Those braces,
Beautiful.

Dear disabled girl
You are a force to be reckoned with;
A wonderful creation

Every imperfection
Is a perfect beauty,
A sign of strength.

Dear disabled girl,
You are so much more
Than disabled,
Dear disabled girl

Onward

by R.S. Rutherford

To the sky, onward to tomorrow
I point my sword, gleaming in the sun
There's a place, where no one's heard of sorrow
We can get there, but we all must run
Hurried feet, dashing 'cross the wasteland
Distant beasts, bellow out their roar
Our hearts beat, like many grains of sand
Our dreams spread wings,
and through the clouds they soar
Though obstacles, may hinder and misplace you
We shall reach, our ever-nearing shore
Through thick and thin, patience is our virtue
Yesterdays are buried, so now let's strive for more
Climb those peaks, higher until morning
Don't look down, though at times we'll fall
Through our strength, we can weather any warning
Your truth lies, in the promise of this all
One more step, stretch out and embrace it
Almost there, no turning back now
Gaze upon, the beauty in this moment
You survived, so go on and take a bow
Stand up proud, atop the strongest mountain

Scream and shout, your voice should be heard
Though our path was grim, our spirit we could count in
So breathe it in, these hopeful, wishful words.

by Malcom Whitby

Uproot the weeding plants that sucks
the nutrients from a budding tree
Stunning its growth, unaware of its potential
Becoming fruitless and seen as useless

Withering away into nothingness
only to be removed and forgotten
to be replaced by another.
What of the soil?

How can we protect these growing souls?
Reeducating their mind? How?

From ground up, reawakening their childish demeanour
Remolding them into a dreamer
erasing degrading scheming.
Refreshing awareness, opening the door to mental
resistance for the media influence

Unlocking a deep awareness to beyond the surface
Washing away the hidden hypnotic messages
Watch for their misleading gesture.

Uproot weeding plants they suck the energy
From a perfectly growing world, rendering the soil
Useless for planting fruitfully and budding flowers
Replenish the soil that which we grow in.

Home
by Sky Boivin

She lays awake

Wrapped in his arms

Listening to the silence

Of the evening night

Such serene calmness

That envelopes her

From such sounds

Nothing happening

In the world

At such hours of the night

She snuggles in more

To his arms

Safe arms

That hold her the night long

As gentle breezes

Kiss their bare skin

Peace and calm

Wash over her

She lays awake

In the arms of home

A Movement
by Rachael DK

It's been months
since so many mobilized,
together in a fashion
some swore
was too radicalized.
The "Ignorance-is-bliss"
approach was trashed.
Resentments surged
over requirements of wearing
a mask.
I've concluded we're
sharing air with people
who hate change.
So, keep on pushing
against the system
that remains.
Final results are what
will really matter.
We could raise the
quality of life,
if we all worked together—
Together in a movement.
A movement bigger than us.

A Better Place To Live in

by Neelam Lashari

Let's save the world
It has the mountains
The trees
The water
The ocean

Let's save the world
It has the stars
The moon
The sun
The planets

Let's save the world
Let's make it beautiful
A better place to live in
A peaceful place to live in

A place where no one
Dies with hunger
No one
Dies with depression
No one

Dies with attacks

No one

Die with unemployment

Let's save the world

Let's make it

A better place

To live in

Let's save the world

It's for you

It's for me

It's for our children

It's for elders

Let's save the world

Let's save the world

Pay It Forward
by Daniel Shatz

When we hold the hand of a child
even for a little while
their hand will roll, and warm the cold
and maybe make them smile

When the young adult is shown what's real
the beauty of nature not the mark of steel
their eyes will hope, and the anger will choke
on it's it's own venomous meal

When we take the hand of the beggar
And feed them till the sadness severs
If they can smile, for a little while
Perhaps it can ease all their endeavours

When we step up and takes five minutes of our day
Instead of looking at a screen wishing it would go away
Those five minutes will multiply by division
And maybe... just maybe forward it will pay

<8.10.20 >

by Sky Boivin

She wakens up to a new day

Hoping for change

She shies away as the day

Grows on

The harshness and

The cruelty that comes

Never failing to creep up

She pushes forward

As best she can

Her mind races on

Bringing what ifs

And more as she gets to thinking

She must not let anyone see

Her weakness deep within

She cries alone

In silence

When in reality

She needs to scream

Until night falls

She holds it all in

Alone where no one else will see

She lays upon her pillow

Allowing tears to silently escape

He returns

Wrapping caring arms

Around her gently

Pushing away all fears

He guards her dreams

Playing soft melodies

To ease away all things

His words of kindness

Bringing her peace

His touch

His arms

wrapped around her

Bringing calm to her mind

All her fears escape her mind

As he quiets her restless

And racing mind

She slumbers more at ease

As he brings peace.

What You Want It To Be
by Norb Aikin

After all,

what do we have to lose?

We live limitless

inside our limits;

deceived into complacency

and rich in what we think

enriches us.

We're not not wrong,

but we're also

very wrong

in playing along

in groups and

societies that

try to angle our functions

to their needs.

And you know and I know

we don't need

those needs.

Pack it in

and unpack;

keep only what you can carry.

None of us is

long for this world;

even more

if we continue longing.

It wasn't built for us

and what exactly

are we trying to build,

if not the same things?

The end is only

the means to more endings.

And the beginning

just leads to more questions

we're yet to see.

Me?

I'm right here...

but I'm not going anywhere.

THANK YOU FOR HELPING US FIGHT HUNGER!

IF YOU LIKED THIS ANTHOLOGY,
PLEASE REVIEW IT ONLINE.

A LOT OF PEOPLE OUT THERE
THANK YOU SO MUCH FOR YOUR HELP.

·

www.ingramcontent.com/pod-product-compliance
Lightning Source LLC
Chambersburg PA
CBHW031219120626
46545CB00003B/915